PLANET DINOSAUR

PLANET DINOSAUR

Steve Parker

Illustrated by
Bob Nicholls

Miles Kelly
PUBLISHING

First published in 2005 by
Miles Kelly Publishing Ltd
Bardfield Centre, Great Bardfield, Essex, CM7 4SL

Copyright © Miles Kelly Publishing Ltd 2005

2 4 6 8 10 9 7 5 3 1

Editorial Director
Belinda Gallagher

Art Director
Jo Brewer

Picture Research Manager
Liberty Newton

Picture Researcher
Laura Faulder

Production
Estela Boulton, Elizabeth Brunwin

Reprographics
Anthony Cambray, Mike Coupe, Stephan Davis, Ian Paulyn

Indexer
Helen Snaith

Artwork
Cover artwork and main scenes illustrated by Bob Nicholls

ISBN 1-84236-563-0

Printed in China

British Library Cataloguing-in-Publication Data
A catalogue record for this book is available
from the British Library

www.mileskelly.net
info@mileskelly.net

All other artworks are from MKP Archives

CONTENTS

PLANET DINOSAUR

Long ago, the world was very different. Reptiles dominated most habitats. They pounded the ground, splashed through water and swooped through the air. This was the Mesozoic Era, 250–65 million years ago (mya). In particular, one group of reptiles ruled the land as no other animals have done before or since – apart, perhaps, from ourselves today. These reptiles included some of the biggest, fastest, heaviest, longest and fiercest creatures ever to have lived. Mesozoic life yielded to their dominance. It was their world – Planet Dinosaur.

For 150 million years, the landscape was filled with dinosaurs and their reptilian cousins, and also strange-looking plants and unfamiliar creatures. Each of this book's five major scenes depicts a particular time span within one of the three periods of the Mesozoic Era: the Triassic, Jurassic and Cretaceous. But Planet Dinosaur offers a different slant on this huge chunk of time. Try to imagine that the dinosaurs ruled the world for just a single day. At 6 AM (220–203 million years ago) the first dinosaurs arrive. By 11 AM (200–160 million years ago), the dinosaurs are flourishing, with bigger and fiercer kinds spreading across the world. At 4 PM (150–135 million years ago) true dinosaur giants are in their element – and the first bird has evolved. By early evening, around 6 PM (120–80 million years ago), there is a change as the carnivores (meat eaters) become more diverse – and deadly. Later that evening, at 8 PM (75–65 million years ago), some of the strangest dinosaurs appear – their time on Earth limited.

Polacanthus
Although covered in bony plates and spikes, the soft, underbelly of this dinosaur made it vulnerable to attack (page 29).

Coelophysis
This speedy dinosaur was a voracious hunter of small prey. It was also the fastest dinosaur on land (page 13).

Saltasaurus
A member of the sauropod group, Saltasaurus was unusual in that its body was covered in bony lumps and plates.

The main scenes pack together dinosaurs and other prehistoric animals that lived at the same time, but often in differing regions, or continents. Discover how dinosaurs moved, fed, bred and escaped – often from each other.

The pages following each scene deal with its main dinosaurs and other animals – size and shape, diet, lifestyle, weaponry and behaviour. There is also information about climate, vegetation, and the positions of the continents as they drifted slowly around the globe. A key at the back will help you to identify each scene's inhabitants. The numbers link to the pages describing the dinosaurs in detail. Why did the dinosaurs disappear? Find out possible reasons for this, and whether today's rulers of Planet Human should look back and learn, to avoid a similar fate.

Maiasaura
The young of Maisaura (above) were possibly the best-cared for dinosaur babies. Fossil evidence supports the fact that these hatchlings were cared for in nurseries.

Spinosaurus

Hammers and teeth
Dinosaurs' weapons included teeth, claws and bony 'hammer' tails. Even herbivores (plant eaters) such as Ankylosaurus could defend themselves against deadly carnivores (meat eaters) such as Spinosaurus (page 30).

Ankylosaurus

The takeover begins

The Triassic Period lasted from 250–203 million years ago. Fossils of the first-known dinosaurs date to the Middle Triassic, about 230 million years ago. As the Period drew to a close, these relatively new creatures were already making their mark. Their upright stance, with legs directly below the body, meant they could run faster and further than their more primitive reptile cousins, whose legs sprawled to the sides. The dinosaurs' race for global supremacy had begun.

Greatest
The Triassic Period began after the greatest mass extinction ever. More than nine-tenths of all kinds of living things disappeared at the end of the preceding Permian Period.

Saltopus [12]
salt-o-pus
Only very few remains of 'leaping foot' have been discovered, near Elgin in Scotland. It was a tiny dinosaur, about the size of a small pet cat. The hands of *Saltopus* had five fingers each, which was a primitive or 'old-fashioned' feature for a meat-eating dinosaur. Over millions of years the number of fingers reduced to three or even two per hand.

Herrerasaurus [4]
herr-ray-rah-SORE-us
Named after Argentinean goat-herder Victorino Herrera, who discovered its fossils, *Herrerasaurus* was a powerful predator up to 4 m long and weighing more than 100 kg. It is one of several very early dinosaurs from about 228 million years ago in what is now South America. In 1988 its almost complete skeleton was unearthed in the foothills of the Andes Mountains near San Juan. The long, narrow jaws were full of sharp, back-curving teeth, and the strong, lengthy rear legs allowed speedy movement.

Ornithosuchus [8]
orn-ITH-oh-sue-kuss
When its fossils were first studied, some experts considered *Ornithosuchus* ('bird crocodile') to be a very early, primitive type of dinosaur. However, it is now classed as a member of a related reptile group, the thecodonts. Some thecodonts may have given rise to the dinosaurs. *Ornithosuchus* was up to 3 m long and had sharp teeth suited to catching big victims and tearing their flesh. It probably ran on all fours or just its rear legs.

Plateosaurus [9]
plat-ee-oh-sore-us
Around 8 m long and weighing perhaps one tonne, *Plateosaurus* was one of the first sizeable dinosaurs. It is well-known from many skeletons unearthed at various sites in Europe, including France, Switzerland and Germany. Its long body, sturdy hips and powerful, weighty tail could mean that it reared up on its hind limbs and leaned back, using its tail as a 'third leg' for support. In this way it reached tree-fern fronds and other plant food 5 m above the ground.

Scaphonyx [13]
SKA-fon-ix

This creature was not a dinosaur, but a member of the group called rhynchosaurs or 'beaked reptiles'. They were plant eaters and ranged from about 2 m in length down to less than 40 cm.

Scaphonyx was one of the larger types, and it used its hooked upper jaw to grab fern-fronds and other ground-level plant growth. Rhynchosaurs were very common at the start of the Age of Dinosaurs but soon faded away, perhaps because the carnivorous dinosaurs found them easy prey.

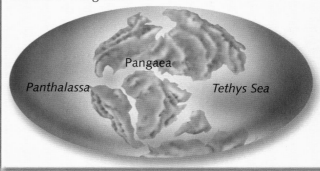

CHANGING CONTINENTS

One land

By the Triassic Period, all of the planet's landmasses had rammed into each other to form the single giant supercontinent known as Pangaea. This arched around an enormous bay, the Tethys Sea, while the superocean Panthalassa, meaning 'all seas', covered the rest of the globe.

Pangaea

Panthalassa   Tethys Sea

Staurikosaurus [14]
stor-ik-oh-sore-us

'Cross reptile' was not annoyed, but named from the Southern Cross pattern of stars seen in the Southern Hemisphere. Its remains come from Brazil, a region with relatively few dinosaur fossils.

They are rare and fragmented, so reconstructions of *Staurikosaurus* are largely intelligent guesswork. It was some 2 m in length and weighed around 15 kg. Its small, pointy teeth were suited to snapping up little prey, from dragonflies to slugs.

Coelophysis [1]
seel-OH-fie-sis

Many dinosaurs are 'rebuilt' on the evidence of just a few scraps of fossilized bone. Not *Coelophysis*, 'hollow form'. Remains of many hundreds of individuals came from a site called Ghost Ranch in New Mexico, USA. The name refers to the birdlike hollow bones that, along with its very slim build, would have made 3-m *Coelophysis* extremely light. Its sharp but small teeth were probably used for grabbing little prey such as bugs and worms, rather than tackling large victims.

Fastest
Coelophysis was probably the fastest land dinosaur of the Triassic Period – in fact, fastest of all animals at the time, with an estimated top speed of 40 km/h.

'Flat reptile'
One of the first really big dinosaurs was Plateosaurus, or 'flat reptile'. Its front feet could be hyper-extended. This flexibility meant that Plateosaurus may have been able to grasp branches while feeding.

Eoraptor [2]
EE-oh-RAP-tor

'Dawn thief' lived at the same time and place as *Herrerasaurus* (page 10). But it was much smaller, only one metre from nose to tail-tip, and would have stood knee-high to an adult. It had unusual leaflike teeth at the front of its mouth, and the more typical meat eater's sharp, curving teeth towards the rear. Light and agile, *Eoraptor* probably grabbed any small creature as prey.

Thecodontosaurus [15]
THEC-o-dont-o-sore-us

Fossils found in England were named as *Thecodontosaurus* in 1843, making this herbivore one of the first few dinosaurs to receive an official scientific name. Its remains are scarce but reveal a long-necked and very long-tailed plant eater, as shown by its small, leaf-shaped teeth. These had serrated (wavy or sawlike) edges for slicing through vegetation. In general shape, *Thecodontosaurus* looked like the later dinosaur giants called sauropods – but it was only 2 m in length.

Riojasaurus [11]
rio-JA-sore-us

One of the first truly large dinosaurs, the remains of *Riojasaurus* date back to 220 million years ago. They were first excavated in the 1960s in the La Rioja district of Argentina, hence the name. Further fossils have been found since of more than 20 individuals. *Riojasaurus* was about 10 m long and weighed more than one tonne. It probably moved on all fours but perhaps reared up on its back legs, like *Plateosaurus* (page 10) , to reach leaves several metres off the ground.

Eudimorphodon [3]
yoo-di-MORPH-o-don

The Mesozoic Era or Age of Dinosaurs could also be called the Age of Pterosaurs. With front legs adapted as long, thin-skinned wings, the first pterosaurs such as *Eudimorphodon* date back 220 million years. The outer part of each wing was held out mainly by the greatly elongated bones of the fourth finger. *Eudimorphodon* had a wing span of about 80 cm and sharp teeth for eating small animals, including fish. Its fossils come from Italy.

Elongated finger bone

Melanorosaurus [6]
mel-uh-NOR-uh-sore-us

Like *Plateosaurus* in Europe (page 10), and *Riojasaurus* in South America, *Melanorosaurus* from southern Africa was a prosauropod – a long-necked, bulky-bodied, long-tailed herbivore. It was named 'Black Mountain reptile' after its discovery site. At a length of around 10 m, its weight was perhaps one tonne or more. This bulk was well supported by four sturdy legs, the rear pair slightly longer than the front.

Earliest?
The oldest-known dinosaur fossils are meat eaters from Argentina and prosauropod plant eaters from Madagascar, around 230 million years ago. But experts believe the group had already become established by then, so even older fossils will be discovered.

CLIMATE AND HABITATS

Desert interior
Around the coastline of the supercontinent Pangaea, warm moisture-laden winds brought rain, which meant that forests began to grow. However, as the winds blew inland, they became drier. This resulted in enormous tracts of Pangaea's interior being nothing more than arid scrubland and desert.

Mussaurus [7]
muss-OR-us

'Mouse reptile' was about 3 m long and weighed twice as much as an adult human. So why the strange name? The first remains of this dinosaur to be studied were babies probably just emerged from their eggs. They were around the size of today's rats and among the smallest of all dinosaur fossils. Only later were parts of the adults discovered. *Mussaurus* lived in what is now Argentina, South America, and fed on low-growing plants such as ferns and horsetails.

Earliest and oldest
Mussaurus is the earliest-known dinosaur baby. Its eggshell fossils represent the oldest-known dinosaur eggs.

Massospondylus [5]
mass-oh-SPON-di-luss

A member of the prosauropod group, *Massospondylus* was about 5 m from nose to tail and slim in build. It is well-known from many fossil discoveries at sites in southeastern and southern Africa. Its name means 'massive vertebrae', referring to the large vertebral bones that made up its spinal column or backbone. Its teeth are unusually long and serrated for a herbivore.

Procompsognathus [10]
pro-comp-sog-nay-thus

The tail of this dinosaur formed almost half of its total length of about 140 cm. It was a slim and agile theropod (member of the meat-eater group), whose fossils come from Germany. Its small teeth were suited to live prey rather than scavenging. The name 'before (pro) *Compsognathus*' is true in that the smaller *Compsognathus* lived later, and the two dinosaurs are similar in shape. But it should not imply that *Compsognathus* was descended from *Procompsognathus*, since a time gap of more than 60 million years separated them.

Thrinaxodon [16]
thrin-AX-o-don

Some reptiles gradually became more mammal-like in their bones and teeth, and also possibly had furry rather than scaly skin. Members of one group, cynodonts, gradually evolved to become the first true mammals. Fossils of the cynodont *Thrinaxodon* come from South Africa. The way its remains were preserved suggest that this cat-sized, very mammal-like reptile may have lived in a burrow.

Earliest
The first mammals appeared at the time of the early dinosaurs, over 210 million years ago. They were small insect eaters, hardly larger than the shrews of today.

Cycads

Most Triassic cycads had an umbrella-like crown of large feathery leaves on a woody, unbranched stem. Some cycads were short and squat, others resembled tall, slim palm trees. They were probably a major food source for medium and large herbivorous dinosaurs such as prosauropods. About 70 types of cycads still grow today, mostly in tropical regions.

Spread and flourish

During the Jurassic Period (203–135 million years ago) dinosaurs spread to all the world's major continents. It also saw the group diversify into new and exciting kinds of many shapes and sizes. Huge, long-necked herbivores were hunted by fierce, powerful carnivores. Smaller plant eaters had bony plates of armour in their skin for defence, or used their fleet-footedness to escape from enemies.

Scutellosaurus [30]
skoo-tell-oh-sore-us

In the Early Jurassic Period, this smallish plant eater scampered across the scrubby landscape of what is now Arizona, USA. It was protected by bony plates called scutes embedded in the skin over its back and sides. *Scutellosaurus* ('little shield reptile') was only 120 cm long and less than 15 kg in weight. It probably used alert agility as well as its defensive armour, leaping away from predators on its long back legs.

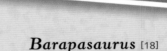

Barapasaurus [18]
bara-pa-SORE-us

Fossils of dinosaurs (and most other animals) are rare in the Indian region. *Barapasaurus* was an Early Jurassic sauropod with the typical long neck, barrel-shaped body and whiplike tail of this plant-eating group. Its fossils were unearthed in the Godavari Valley in southern India and make up parts of six skeletons, but without any foot or skull bones. At 18–20 m long, this herbivore probably weighed more than 25 tonnes and perhaps as much as 40 tonnes.

Thighs
The thigh bone or femur of Barapasaurus was as tall as an adult person, at about 170 cm.

Barosaurus [19]
BAR-oh-sore-us

From the Late Middle Jurassic, *Barosaurus* had an enormously long, strong neck and tail, but a relatively small body. Its total length was about 25 m, and it weighed in the region of 30 tonnes. The neck had 16–17 cervical vertebrae or neck bones, some almost one metre in length. Remains of this sauropod, or long-necked plant eater, have been identified at many excavations in Utah and South Dakota, USA, and possibly in Tanzania, east Africa.

CHANGING CONTINENTS

Cracks appear

By the Middle Jurassic Period, Pangaea had begun to break apart. The chief northern landmass was Laurasia, consisting of future North America, Europe and Asia. The southern continents were grouped as Gondwana. Changing sea levels meant the outlines of these continents were very different from their shapes today.

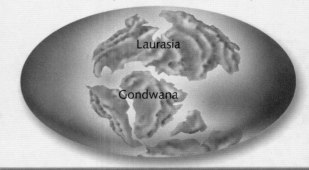

Laurasia

Gondwana

Shunosaurus [32]
SHOON-oh-SORE-us

A smaller sauropod from the Middle
Jurassic, *Shunosaurus* had
the typical long neck,
bulky body and long
tail of its group.
It was about 11 m
long and probably
weighed more than
10 tonnes. Its most
noticeable feature was a tail club
made of enlarged end-of-tail
bones, possibly armed with
several spikes. This would be an
effective defensive weapon
when swung at marauding
carnivores.

Tail club

Teeth
Two fossilized *Lesothosaurus*
were found as if curled up in a
burrow, together with teeth that
they may have lost or shed –
they could have been hibernating
to avoid the drought period.

Skulls
Remains of *Shunosaurus* include
five skulls, which is unusual since
the skull is among the smallest,
most fragile part of a sauropod's
body, and rarely fossilizes.

Lesothosaurus [25]
Le-so-toe-sore-us

'Lesotho reptile' was about
one metre or so in length and
stood only half that in height.
Its fossils come from southern
Africa. The proportionally long
shins and toes, compared to the thighs, show that this
was a very speedy little creature. It would dash away
from danger in the manner of a modern-day small deer
or gazelle. Its sharp-edged teeth fitted closely together
to slice through tough plant food.

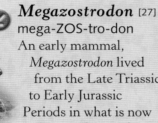

Megazostrodon [27]
mega-ZOS-tro-don

An early mammal,
Megazostrodon lived
from the Late Triassic
to Early Jurassic
Periods in what is now
Lesotho, southern Africa
(see *Lesothosaurus*, above). At 12 cm
long, it could have easily crouched on a human hand. Its
large eyes and long snout were perfectly adapted for seeing
and sniffing in the darkness, as it searched for meals of
grubs and bugs. It seized prey with its sharp front teeth
and chewed with its wider back teeth.

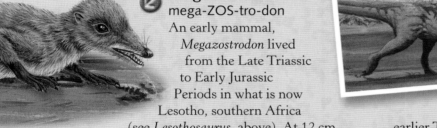

Yunnanosaurus [33]
yoo-NAN-oh-sore-us

Named after its discovery
region of Yunnan, China,
this plant eater was
probably a member of
the prosauropod group
of dinosaurs, like
Plateosaurus (page 10)
and *Riojasaurus* (page 12) from the
earlier Triassic Period. Teeth found with its fossil bones
are spoon-shaped, rather than leaflike as in typical
prosauropods, but they may be from another dinosaur
entirely. *Yunnanosaurus* dates from the Early Jurassic, was
about 7 m in length, and spent most of its time swinging
its neck around to crop leaves and fronds.

Dilophosaurus [21]
die-LOAF-oh-sore-us

At 6 m in length and half a tonne in weight,
Dilophosaurus was one of the earliest sizeable
theropods or meat-eating dinosaurs. Its fossils are
known from Arizona, USA, and Yunnan, China. It was
a lithe and agile hunter with sharp, curved fangs, easily
able to run down prey such as the newly hatched
young of herbivorous sauropods. It was named
'two ridge reptile' after the head crest, consisting
of two narrow, curved plates of bone projecting
from the forehead – like half dinner-plates
stuck into its head! The crest may have
been a sign of maturity and readiness to
breed, or a feature that distinguished
between males and females.

Head crest

Megalosaurus [26]
MEG-ah-low-sore-us

'Big reptile' was a large theropod, or predatory dinosaur, from the Middle Jurassic Period. In the early days of digging up fossils and naming dinosaurs, during the middle to late 19th century, almost any discovery with big, sharp teeth was labelled *Megalosaurus* – including *Eustreptospondylus* (below). Only later did experts appreciate there were many kinds of large carnivorous dinosaurs and begin to give them separate names. This dinosaur was probably about 9 m long and most of its remains come from England.

First name

Megalosaurus was the first dinosaur to receive an official scientific name, in 1824. That was 18 years before the name 'dinosaur' itself was coined for this group of reptiles.

Heterodontosaurus [24]
HET-er-oh-DONT-oh-sore-us

Most reptiles, including most dinosaurs, had teeth of much the same shape all along their jaws. 'Different-tooth reptile' was named after its three kinds of teeth. These included sharp front teeth in the upper jaw, for cutting off plant food against a horny pad at the front of the lower jaw. Behind them were two pairs of long, fanglike teeth, each pair fitting into grooved sockets in the opposite jaw. At the back were flatter, broader teeth for crushing. The tusklike fangs may have been used for defence or for battling against rivals at breeding time. *Heterodontosaurus* was about 120 cm long and lived from the Late Triassic to Early Jurassic Periods in southern Africa.

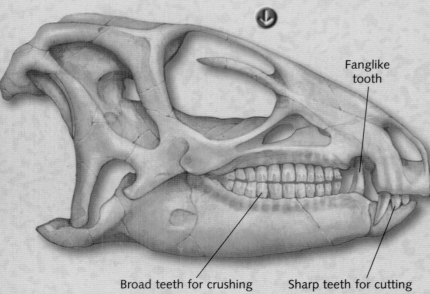

Fanglike tooth

Broad teeth for crushing   Sharp teeth for cutting

Anchisaurus [17]
ANK-ee-sore-us

Little more than 2 m long, *Anchisaurus* or 'near reptile' was one of the smallest prosauropods or long-necked plant eaters. Its fossils were discovered in the Connecticut Valley of Massachusetts, USA. This dinosaur could bound along on all fours or rear up to sprint on its back legs.

Unidentified
Fossils of Anchisaurus were the first to be scientifically described in North America, in 1818. But they were first thought to be of human origin, and not identified as a dinosaur until 1912.

Cetiosaurus [20]
CEE-TEE-oh-sore-us

The name *Cetiosaurus*, 'whale reptile', came about because the fossil backbones (vertebrae) from this dinosaur were originally identified as from a whale. This Middle Jurassic sauropod showed a mix of features from earlier prosauropods and later, even greater sauropod plant eaters. At 25 tonnes in weight, and about 15 m in length, *Cetiosaurus* remains have been associated with water plants and animals. It may have lived in swamps and munched soft-leaved aquatic vegetation.

Eustreptospondylus [23]
ewe-strep-toe-SPON-die-lus

In the Middle Jurassic Period, this fierce predator roamed near what is now Oxford, England. Much larger than its equivalent carnivores today, the big cats, *Eustreptospondylus* was 7 m long and weighed a quarter of a tonne. It ran speedily on its strong back legs and four-toed feet, although only three toes touched the ground. The large head contained long jaws filled with sharp, serrated-edged teeth. Its name, 'well-curved vertebra', refers to the shape of the joint surfaces on its backbones.

Dimorphodon [22]
DIE-more-foe-don

The pterosaur *Dimorphodon* had a nose-to-tail length of about one metre, and a wing span of 140 cm. Its fossils from southern England include a deep, beaklike mouth with small but sharp teeth, ideally suited for grabbing fish. Like other early pterosaurs, *Dimorphodon* had a long tail, which probably worked as a rudder for steering in flight.

Seismosaurus [31]
SIZE-moh-SORE-us

This huge sauropod is sometimes hailed as the longest of all dinosaurs. However, estimates of 50–55 m from nose to tail-tip are based on only partial fossils. Alternative guesses are as 'short' as 35 m – which still far exceeds the biggest creature of today, the blue whale. Remains of *Seismosaurus* were found in New Mexico, USA. It was named 'earthquake reptile' from the idea that the ground shook as it lumbered along, although later sauropods such as *Brachiosaurus* (page 22) and *Argentinosaurus* (page 29) were probably more than twice as heavy.

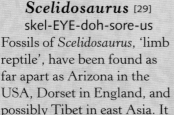

Horselike
Rhoetosaurus was named after a hero from ancient Greek myth, Rhoetus, who was a centaur – half-human, half-horse.

Rhoetosaurus [28]
REE-tuh-sore-us

One of the first Australian dinosaurs to be named, *Rhoetosaurus* has many similarities to its sauropod cousin *Shunosaurus* (page 17). Its fossils come from Roma, Queensland, and show a robust-bodied plant eater about 15 m in length and 15 tonnes in weight.

CLIMATE AND HABITATS

Warm and wetter
During the Jurassic Period, the climate gradually became damper. This was partly the result of Pangaea splitting, which meant more regions were nearer the coast with its moisture-rich winds. Forests of conifers, gingkoes and tree-ferns spread into areas that were formerly Triassic deserts.

Scelidosaurus [29]
skel-EYE-doh-sore-us

Fossils of *Scelidosaurus*, 'limb reptile', have been found as far apart as Arizona in the USA, Dorset in England, and possibly Tibet in east Asia. It was one of the early kinds of armoured dinosaurs known as thyreophorans or 'shield-bearers', which later included ankylosaurs and stegosaurs. *Scelidosaurus* had many bony knobs, cones and ridges over its back and sides. It was about 4 m long, lived during the Early–Middle Jurassic Period and nipped off plant food with its beaklike mouth.

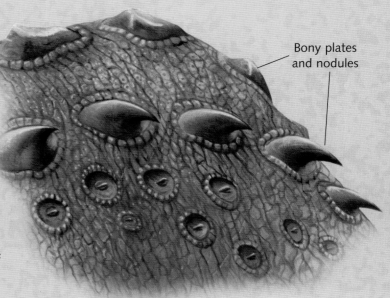

Bony plates and nodules

Land of the giants

The Late Jurassic Period, about 150 million years ago, boasts more huge dinosaurs than any other time. Biggest were the sauropods or 'lizard-feet' – giants like Brachiosaurus, Apatosaurus, Mamenchisaurus *and* Diplodocus. *Lush forests of trees and huge ferns provided plentiful food for these massive monsters. There were mini-dinosaurs too, including one of the smallest of all,* Compsognathus. *A new shape was in the sky – the first bird,* Archaeopteryx.

Hollow bones

Neck-iest
The neck of Mamenchisaurus was up to 15 m long, and had up to 19 cervical vertebrae (neck bones). This title of 'longest neck' was recently challenged by Sauroposeidon (page 27).

Mamenchisaurus [44]
mah-men-chi-sore-us
One of the longest necks of all time belonged to 'Mamen ferry reptile', named after a waterway crossing in China where its fossils were first discovered. At 25 m in length, this plant eater weighed perhaps 20 tonnes. However, the structure of the neck bones and the joints between them suggests that this sauropod could not raise its neck very high. Instead, it probably stood in one place and swung its head around in a great arc, keeping its neck parallel to the ground as it raked in the leaves of fairly low-growing plants.

Brachiosaurus [37]
BRAK-ee-oh-sore-us
Despite scattered fossil finds from other immense sauropods, *Brachiosaurus* is still the biggest dinosaur known from fairly complete remains. It was also one of the most widespread, living in Africa, Europe and North America. At 25 m long, estimates of its weight range from 30–75 tonnes. *Brachiosaurus* means 'arm lizard' and refers to the greatly elongated front legs. Along with its flagpole-length neck, this meant *Brachiosaurus* could reach food 14 m from the ground.

Camarasaurus [38]
KAM-ar-a-SORE-us
'Chambered reptile' was certainly big, at 20 m in length and 20 tonnes in weight. But its neck and tail were proportionally shorter and thicker than many of its immense sauropod cousins. Like many other sauropods, the first toe (digit one) had a long, sharp claw rather than the nail or hooflike claws on the other toes. It was probably used as a defensive weapon. Its fossils have been recovered from several US states including Colorado, Wyoming, Utah and New Mexico.

Sharp claw for defence

Compsognathus [41]
KOMP-sog-NATH-us
Compsognathus ('pretty jaw') is the smallest dinosaur known from fairly complete fossils. Not much longer than a pet cat, it weighed just 2 kg. Its back legs were not much thicker than your thumbs, its front legs were pencil-slim, and half its length was composed of a whippy tail. But this little dinosaur, a member of the coelurosaur group, was a fierce predator of small prey such as insects, worms, lizards, and perhaps newly hatched baby dinosaurs. Its fossils in Germany come from the same time and region as those of the bird *Archaeopteryx*.

Missing clues
Brachiosaurus, like many dinosaurs, is depicted with flaps of skin on its neck, back and tail. Early fossil studies missed these faint impressions. It's now thought that many dinosaurs had these adornments.

Kentrosaurus [43]
ken-TROH-sore-us

The plant-nipping 'beak', low-slung head, arched back with projecting bony plates, and spiky tail show that *Kentrosaurus* was a member of the stegosaur group. Indeed, its name means 'spiked reptile'. Its fossils, along with those of *Brachiosaurus* and many others, were unearthed at a famous site called Tendaguru in what is now Tanzania, east Africa. *Kentrosaurus* was more than one tonne in weight and 5 m in length.

Wing span
Different types of Rhamphorhynchus had wing spans ranging from less than 40 cm to more than 170 cm.

Rhamphorhynchus [46]
ram-FOR-rin-kus

This long-tailed pterosaur had a slim, pointed beak with thin fanglike teeth sticking out at odd angles. It probably swooped over water to grab fish and other swimmers near the surface. Many fossils of up to seven different types of *Rhamphorhynchus* have been uncovered in Germany (including the Solnhofen region where *Archaeopteryx* remains were found), England, Portugal and other sites in Europe, and also east Africa.

Nostrils
There seems to be no reason for the position of the nostrils of Brachiosaurus – rather than at the front of its snout, they were on top of its arched head.

Ornitholestes [45]
or-ni-tho-LES-tees

'Bird robber' was named because the first experts to study its fossils, about 100 years ago, imagined it chasing and killing birds for food. Its long, powerful arms and hands were tipped with curved claws like bent daggers – ideal for grabbing small prey. The rear legs and tail were long too, and the slim, light build gave a total weight of just 15 kg for this dinosaur's 2-m length.

CHANGING CONTINENTS

The split continues
Pangaea was well on the way to splitting up by the Late Jurassic Period. Seas had flooded northern areas, dividing North America from Asia. In Gondwana to the south, Africa and South America were still side by side, with Australia, Antarctica and India forming a chain of landmasses towards the east.

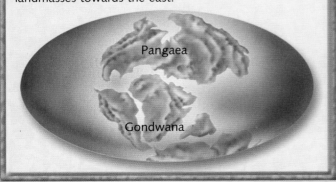

Pangaea

Gondwana

Allosaurus [34]
AL-oh-sore-us

The vast sauropods were the biggest-ever meals on four legs. Great predators took advantage of these meat-mountains. The largest predator in the Late Jurassic was *Allosaurus*, 'different/strange reptile'. At 12 m long and 2-plus tonnes in weight, it almost rivalled the great *Tyrannosaurus*, although it lived 70 million years earlier. The Cleveland–Lloyd Dinosaur Quarry in Utah, USA, was once a death trap for these huge hunters. Other dinosaurs became stuck in what looked like a pool but was in fact thick mud. Passing *Allosaurus* tried to eat them but were sucked under. This happened year after year – so far, remains have been found of more than 65 *Allosaurus*.

Coelurus [40]
seel-YEW-rus

A smallish predator about 2 m in length, *Coelurus* was named 'hollow form' after its tubelike limb and tail bones. The spaces in the bones helped to save weight so that this slim, agile meat eater was just 15 kg. Its fossils come from Wyoming, USA and it has given its name to a general group of smallish, speedy carnivores, the coelurosaurs. These probably chased or scrabbled in the soil for small prey such as lizards, worms, grubs and insects.

Archaeopteryx [36]
ark-ee-OPT-er-ix

Despite many counter-claims, 'ancient wing' is still the first-known bird. It lived during the Late Jurassic Period in what is now southern Germany. It was slightly larger than a chicken and a curious mixture of reptile – with teeth in its jaws and a long bony tail – and bird, with its feathers and winglike front limbs. *Archaeopteryx* was probably a reasonable flier – its feathers were not simply for warmth, but had the same detailed design for flight found on birds today. It probably fed on insects, grubs, lizards and other small creatures.

Apatosaurus [35]
ah-PAT-oh-sore-us

At 23 m and 30-plus tonnes, 'deceptive reptile' *Apatosaurus* may not be as famous as another sauropod, the 'thunder reptile' *Brontosaurus*. Yet the two are the same beast. In the rush to discover and name as many dinosaurs as possible, the first of its fossil remains were called *Apatosaurus* in 1877. In 1879 similar remains were unearthed and called *Brontosaurus*, a name that caught the public's imagination. However, many years later, it was agreed that these sets of fossils represented the same beast. So by scientific tradition, the first name was kept and *Brontosaurus* was removed from the official list of dinosaurs.

Tail-iest
The tail of Apatosaurus contained about 82 bones (caudal vertebrae) – even more than the longer tail of Diplodocus. It could probably 'snap' like a whip with power at enemies.

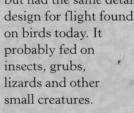

Tuojiangosaurus [48]
too-YANG-oh-sore-us

Named after the Tuo River in China, this 7 m, one-tonne plant eater was a member of the stegosaur group. It showed how the stegosaurs had spread to most continents by the Late Jurassic Period, with *Stegosaurus* itself living in North America. Like other group members, *Tuojiangosaurus* had tall triangles or leaf-shaped plates of bone along its back. These were probably arranged sticking upright in two rows. The birdlike beak cropped low vegetation, and the four large spikes at the end of the tail were arranged as two V-shapes in a formidable defensive weapon.

Head-less
The heads of sauropods such as Apatosaurus were relatively tiny – hardly larger than the head of a modern pony.

Diplodocus [42]
DI-plod-oh-kuss

Extremely long at 27 m, *Diplodocus* was relatively light for a Late Jurassic sauropod, at 12–15 tonnes. Its name, meaning 'double beam', refers to skilike bony 'skids' on the undersides of its tail bones. *Diplodocus* lived in the Midwest of North America and raked leaves from twigs with a fringe of peglike teeth at the front of its mouth.

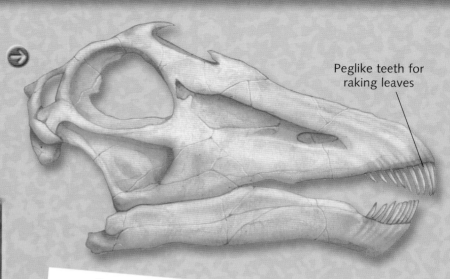

Peglike teeth for raking leaves

CLIMATE AND HABITATS

Green was the colour

The climate about 150 million years ago was warm and wet almost everywhere. It encouraged luxuriant tall forests of tree-ferns, conifers, gingkoes and palmlike cycads, while mosses, horsetails and ferns carpeted the ground. Enormous sauropod dinosaurs browsed at all levels, from treetops down to the ground.

Stomach stones

Piles of rounded, smoothly polished stones, up to the size of soccer balls, are often found with the remains of huge plant eaters such as Brachiosaurus and Diplodocus. The likely explanation is that these are gastroliths or 'stomach stones'. The dinosaurs swallowed them deliberately to help grind up their mountainous meals of plant food. In the process the stones became smooth and shiny, as if in a grinding mill.

Gingkoes

Also known as maidenhair trees, gingkoes were very common during the Jurassic Period. Along with conifers such as pines and redwoods, they formed vast forests in the lush landscape, and their fan-shaped leaves fed many huge herbivorous dinosaurs. Today only one kind of gingko survives. It came originally from China but is now planted as a park and garden tree in most regions.

Tallest
Sauroposeidon may have stood 16 m or more tall – three times the height of today's record holder, the giraffe.

Sauroposeidon [47]
SORE-oh-pos-eye-don

'Reptile of Poseidon' was named after the mythical Greek god of the sea (and earthquakes!). It was a cousin of *Brachiosaurus* (page 22), with front legs much longer than rear limbs – the reverse of the pattern in most of the giant sauropods. Its fossils are nowhere near as complete as those for *Brachiosaurus*. But if estimates are correct, *Sauroposeidon* may have been even taller than its relative, and almost as heavy, at 50-plus tonnes. Its remains were found in Oklahoma, USA, and date from the Late Jurassic or Early Cretaceous Period.

Ceratosaurus [39]
sir-RAT-oh-sore-us

Named after the rhino-like projection on its snout, 'horn reptile' also had a jutting bony ridge above each eye. This theropod (meat eater) was about 6 m long and weighed almost one tonne. It lived around the same time and in the same region of North America as the even larger *Allosaurus* (page 23). In fact their fossils have been found together in the same quarries.

New directions

At the end of the Jurassic Period, about 135 million years ago, a great change overtook the dinosaurs. Many of the huge sauropods disappeared from lands where they had been so common. During the early part of the Cretaceous Period the ornithopods or 'bird-feet', typified by Iguanodon, quickly became the main plant eaters. The carnivores were also becoming more varied, with many smaller but equally deadly types such as Deinonychus and other 'raptors'. And new colours dotted the landscape – flowering plants had arrived.

Giganotosaurus [54]
gig-an-OH-toe-SORE-us

For almost 100 hundred years, *Tyrannosaurus* from the Late Cretaceous Period held the honour of being the largest meat eater ever to walk the Earth. In 1994 all that changed when fossils of an even greater carnivore were discovered in the Patagonia region of Argentina. Named *Giganotosaurus*, 'giant southern reptile', this theropod was up to 14 m in length and weighed possibly 8 tonnes. Its puny arms had three-fingered hands and its teeth, shaped like arrowheads, were more than 20 cm in length. This biggest of land predators preyed on the huge sauropod dinosaurs.

Stegosaurus [65]
STEG-oh-SORE-us

One of the enduring puzzles about dinosaurs is the reason for the tall, diamond-shaped back plates of *Stegosaurus*, 'roof reptile'. They were made of lightweight bone, probably covered by skin in life, and little use for protection. Perhaps they worked as heat-absorbers to soak up the sun's warmth so that this herbivore could get moving more quickly in the morning than other cold-blooded dinosaurs. *Stegosaurus* measured about 9 m from nose to tail and weighed 3 tonnes. Its fossils date to Late Jurassic and Early Cretaceous times.

Big-head

The skull of Giganotosaurus measured over 180 cm – as long as an adult person is high.

Spinosaurus [64]
SPIN-oh-SORE-us

A huge meat eater almost as big as *Tyrannosaurus* (page 34), 'spiny reptile' lived in North Africa and had a long, low, crocodile-like head similar to that of *Baryonyx* (page 29). It has given its name to a group of theropod dinosaurs, the spinosaurs. *Spinosaurus* also had a distinctive 'sail' on its back, formed of skin held up by long bony rods – neural spines that projected from its vertebrae (backbones). The sail was almost 2 m tall. It may have been a temperature regulator, working in a similar way to the back plates of *Stegosaurus*, described above.

Baryonyx [50]
bah-ree-ON-ix
Long, lean and lithe, the carnivore *Baryonyx* was named 'heavy claw' from the massive curved claw on the first digit or thumb of each front limb. Fossils associated with *Baryonyx* include many fish scales, so this hunter may have lurked in swamps and hooked up fish to eat with its long, low, crocodile-like jaws and teeth. *Baryonyx* was about 10 m in length and about 2 tonnes in weight.

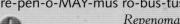

Thumb claw for catching fish

Stabbing claw for defence

Iguanodon [56]
ig-WHA-noh-don
'Iguana tooth' is one of the best-studied dinosaurs, since so many of its fossils have been found across Europe. One coal mine in Belgium yielded the remains of about 40 almost complete skeletons jumbled together. This suggests a herd of *Iguanodon* perished, perhaps while trying to cross a river. On each 'thumb' (first front toe) *Iguanodon* had a spike for jabbing enemies. In early reconstructions of *Iguanodon*, the spike was placed on its nose. *Iguanodon* weighed around 4–5 tonnes, about the same as an African elephant, and was up to 10 m long.

Official
Iguanodon was the second dinosaur to receive an official scientific name, in 1825.

Beaky
Iguanodon nipped off food with the toothless 'beak' at the front of its mouth, and ground it up with its broad, ridged cheek teeth, each about the size of a thumb.

Polacanthus [61]
pol-a-KAN-thus
One of the early armoured dinosaurs or ankylosaurs, 'many spines' was a lumbering herbivore about 5 m long. The layout of its protective spikes is not clear, but they may have jutted from the shoulders. It is not certain whether *Polacanthus* had a tail club for swinging at enemies. Its fossils have been found in southern England and at various sites on mainland Europe.

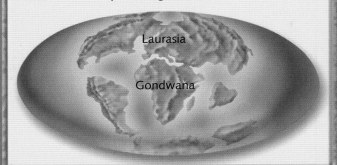

Repenomamus robustus [63]
re-pen-o-MAY-mus ro-bus-tus

Repenomamus robustus, or 'strong reptile-mammal', was more than 50 cm in length and weighed 4–6 kg. It was about the size of a modern opossum. Although clearly a mammal, the teeth were pointed and the limbs stuck out at an angle, similar to that of reptiles. This creature probably preyed on small or young dinosaurs.

CHANGING CONTINENTS

Broken and scattered
During the first part of the Cretaceous Period, the two multi-continents of Laurasia and Gondwana finally fragmented to give the main landmasses we know today. However, sea levels were high, so less land was exposed, mainly as several huge 'islands' that changed their size and shape through time.

Laurasia

Gondwana

Argentinosaurus [49]
AR-gent-eeno-sore-us
Named after its country of discovery, this vast reptile is probably the largest dinosaur and biggest land animal known from fossils. It belonged to the sauropod group called titanosaurs, which were found mainly in the southern continents, and differed from the earlier sauropods, such as diplodocids, in North America. Remains of *Argentinosaurus* are nowhere near as complete as for its main rival in size, record-holder *Brachiosaurus* (page 22). But they suggest *Argentinosaurus* was about 40 m in length and approaching 100 tonnes in weight.

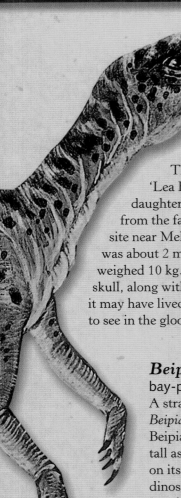

Leaellynasaura [57]
LEE-ELL-IN-a-sore-a
This small plant eater was named 'Lea Ellyn's reptile' after the young daughter of its discoverers. Its fossils come from the famous 'Dinosaur Cove' coastal cliff site near Melbourne, Australia. *Leaellynasaura* was about 2 m long, 50 cm tall at the hips, and weighed 10 kg. The large orbits (eye sockets) in its skull, along with plant fossils from the site, suggest it may have lived in thick forest and so had big eyes to see in the gloom.

Beipiaosaurus [51]
bay-pie-ow-SORE-us
A strange recent find from China, *Beipiaosaurus* was named after the city of Beipiao near its fossil site. It was about as tall as a person and had very long claws on its front limbs, placing it in the dinosaur group called therizinosaurs or 'scythe reptiles'. Fossil impressions show filament-like 'feathers' covering its limbs, and perhaps its body too. *Beipiaosaurus* probably ate plant foods, but its way of life is still very much a mystery.

Longest
Some therizinosaur dinosaurs had thumb claws that were longer than an adult human's arm.

Flowering plants
Flowering plants (angiosperms) dominate the land today – flowers, herbs, blossoms and broadleaved trees. They first appeared during the Early Cretaceous Period, more than 100 million years ago. Their blooms not only brought new colours but also new sources of food for plant-eating dinosaurs and other herbivores. This may have led to the rise of new dinosaur groups like the ornithopods. Cretaceous flowering plants included ancient versions of magnolias (left), laurels, waterlilies, maples, sycamores, walnuts and oaks.

Psittacosaurus [62]
SIT-a-koh-sore-us
In 2004 an amazing discovery in China showed the remains of an adult *Psittacosaurus*, a small parrot-beaked plant eater, surrounded by about 34 young or juveniles. This suggests the adult was caring for the youngsters in a crèche or nursery, when they all perished in a sudden disaster. *Psittacosaurus* was an early type of horned dinosaur, or ceratopsian, about 2 m long, whose fossils come from east Asia.

Caudipteryx [52]
caw-dip-ter-ix
Caudipteryx, 'tail feather', was probably a dinosaur with various bird features. It had a beak, feathers on its body and front limbs, and a long, feathered tail. But its front limbs were not wings for flying, so why have feathers? Reasons include insulation to keep in body warmth (implying that it was warm-blooded), and for colourful displays to mates at breeding time. *Caudipteryx* was about the size of a turkey and its fossils come from China.

Deinonychus [53]
die-NON-i-kuss

'Terrible claw' was named after the sharp, curving claw on the second toe of each foot. The joints in the toe allowed the claw to be held off the ground when walking and running, to keep it sharp. Then it could be swung fast in an arc with a slashing motion, to attack victims. *Deinonychus* fossils have been found in groups, suggesting this dinosaur was a pack-hunter. It grew to 3 m long and weighed about as much as an adult human.

Iberomesornis [55]
i-BERO-me-SOR-nis

Slightly larger than a sparrow, this well-feathered bird was an able flier. But it had some 'old-fashioned' reptile features, such as a claw on the front of each wing and small, spikelike teeth in its beak. Its fossils come from Las Hoyas, Spain. *Iberomesornis* was probably an omnivore, eating whatever it could find. Its remains were preserved as part of a lake bed, so it may have 'fished' for small water creatures such as freshwater shrimps.

CLIMATE AND HABITATS

Settled seasons

The Cretaceous Period saw seasonal changes become more marked, with warm summers and cool winters away from the tropics, rather than constant year-round temperatures. Also, some equatorial areas became drier. The result was more varied habitats, encouraging plants and animals to adapt to new surroundings.

Ornithodesmus [60]
orn-ITH-oh-DES-mus

From the Late Jurassic Period a new group of pterosaurs appeared – the pterodactyloids. Unlike the earlier rhamphorhynchoids they had very short or no tails, and many had bony projections or crests from the skull. They included *Ornithodesmus*, whose fossils were found on the Isle of Wight, southern England. This big, strong flier had wings spanning 5 m and a large ducklike bill studded with small sharp teeth, for gripping slippery prey such as fish.

Minmi [59]
min-mie

Named after a small settlement near its discovery site in Queensland, Australia, *Minmi* was a small ankylosaur (armoured dinosaur). Its body was protected by plates and knobs of bone embedded in thick, tough, leathery skin. *Minmi* was about 3 m long and one metre tall at its humped back. It moved slowly on all fours, cropped plant food with its toothless 'beak', and swung its long and powerful tail at enemies.

First
A fossil bone and eggshell of *Maiasaura* were the first dinosaur remains in space, on the US Spacelab 2 mission in 1985.

Maiasaura [58]
my-ah SORE-ah

This Mid–Late Cretaceous plant eater was a hadrosaur or 'duckbill' dinosaur. It grew to 9 m in length and weighed around 3–4 tonnes. In the 1970s, huge collections of *Maiasaura* skeletons of all ages, from babies to adults, were found in Montana, USA. They showed that these dinosaurs bred in colonies, and each laid its eggs in a nest scooped out of earth. The teeth of the babies were worn from eating, yet their limb bones were not well enough developed for walking. The parent dinosaur may have brought food to them in the nest, hence the name, which means 'good mother reptile'.

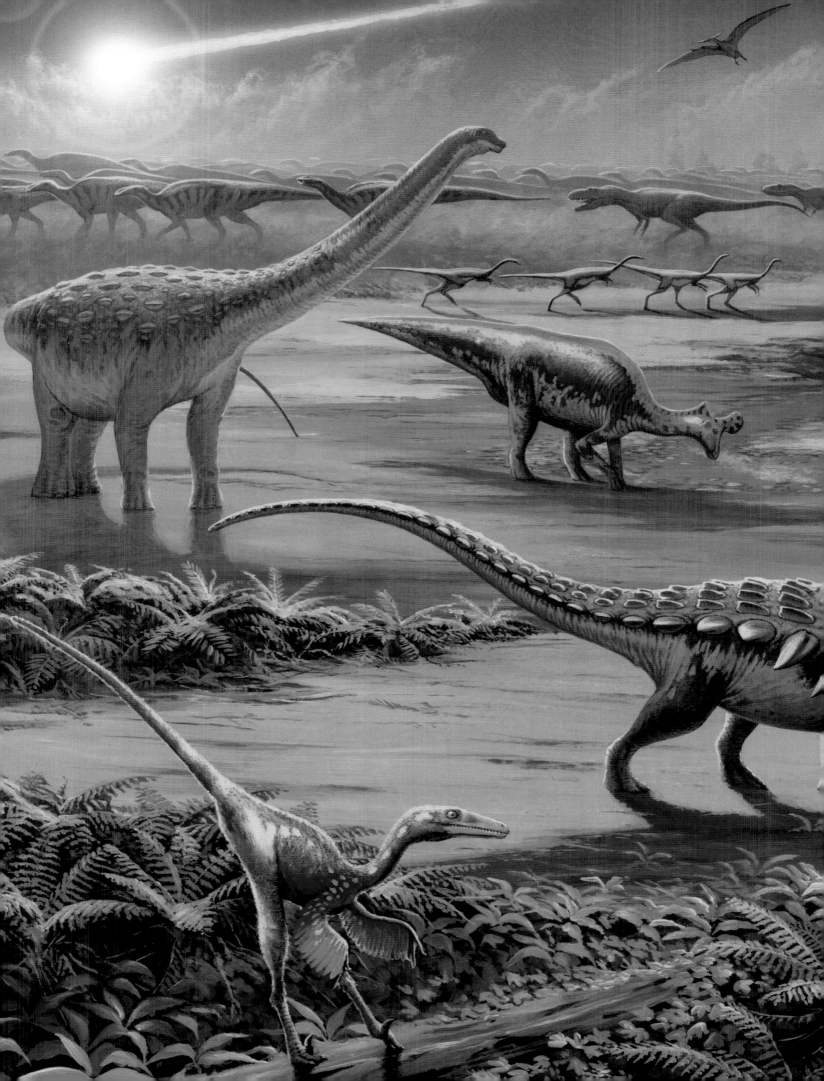

The last hours

The Late Cretaceous Period, around 70–65 million years ago, saw some of the strangest of all dinosaurs. Success stories included the hadrosaurs or duckbilled dinosaurs – whose fossils have been found by the thousands – and the slim, speedy ornithomimosaurs or ostrich-dinosaurs. But in a very short time, all the dinosaurs would be gone, along with the pterosaurs, many sea reptiles, shellfish and numerous plants, too. Planet Dinosaur was about to end. The way would be clear for the next dominant group of creatures. The world would soon become Planet Mammal.

Edmontosaurus [70]
ed-MON-toe-sore-us

One of the largest hadrosaurs, or duckbills, 'Edmonton reptile' (from Edmonton, Canada) was 15 m long and weighed around four tonnes – as much as a large African elephant. The shape of the nose bone suggests *Edmontosaurus* may have had a loose 'bag' of skin on its snout, which it could inflate like a balloon, perhaps as a visual sign to mates or rivals when breeding, or to make a trumpeting call.

Zalambdalestes [82]
za-lam-da-LEST-ees

Only 20 cm in length, this little mammal lived near the end of the Cretaceous Period in what is now Mongolia. It had long rear legs for leaping, an elongated snout to sniff for food, and large eyes. It probably came out at night to avoid the smaller hunting dinosaurs, and scrabbled in soil for insects and similar prey.

Tyrannosaurus [81]
tie-RAN-oh-sore-us

Famed as the biggest hunting animal to walk the land, 'tyrant reptile' has lost this record to *Giganotosaurus* (page 28). However *Tyrannosaurus* remains the dinosaur we love to fear. It was up to 13 m long, 6 m in height, and 6 tonnes in weight. The 50 or so teeth grew to 30 cm in length and *Tyrannosaurus'* mouth opened so wide that it could easily have swallowed a 10-year-old child. This great predator lived in North America and was one of the last dinosaurs.

Neck frill

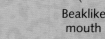

Beaklike mouth

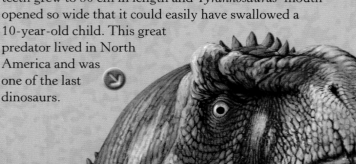

Triceratops [79]
tri-SERRA-tops

Biggest of the horned dinosaurs or ceratopsians, 'three horned face' was no easy victim to predators such as *Tyrannosaurus*. Its eyebrow horns were almost one metre long and its wide, bony neck frill was larger than a dining table. At 9 m long and weighing over 5 tonnes, *Triceratops* would have charged with twice the bulk and power of today's rhinoceros. But most of the time it probably snipped off vegetation with its sharp parrot-like beak, and munched this food with its many sharp-ridged cheek teeth.

Troodon [80]
TROH-oh-don
This big-brained theropod dinosaur was a slender, lightweight hunter of small lizards, birds, mammals and other little prey. Its fossils from North America show that its eyes were large, and from the shape of the brain cavity inside the skull, it had keen senses of sight, hearing and smell. *Troodon* was about 3 m from nose to tail, would have stood chest-high to a person and weighed some 50 kg. Its name means 'wounding tooth'.

Least
Troodon was named in 1856 from the evidence of just one fossil tooth.

Brainiest
The dinosaur with the largest brain compared to its body size was Troodon. Its brain-body ratio was similar to that of birds such as parrots.

Saltasaurus [75]
salt-a-sore-us
One of the last of the great 'long-necks' or sauropods, *Saltasaurus* lived in what is now Argentina. It is unusual for this group of herbivores in possessing protective bony lumps and plates in its skin, ranging from the size of a human hand down to as small as shirt buttons. About 12 m long, *Saltasaurus* is named after the region where its fossils were discovered, Salta Province.

Bony lumps and plates on body

Parasaurolophus [73]
pa-ra-saw-ROL-off-us
Of the many kinds of hadrosaurs (duckbilled dinosaurs), the longest head crest belonged to *Parasaurolophus*. This extraordinary structure projected up and back from the skull for almost 2 m. It was not solid bone, but contained two air tubes that led from the nostrils, passed up inside the front of the crest, looped over at the top and then passed down again, on the way to the lungs. The dinosaur may have been able to blow air through its crest to make a low honking sound, like a trombone or even a fog-horn. *Parasaurolophus* was about 12 m long and weighed 2–3 tonnes.

CHANGING CONTINENTS

Familiar ground
The continents continued to slide to the positions we see today (below) as the Atlantic Ocean widened. The subcontinent of India was far to the south, near Africa. It would take millions of years to drift northeast and ram into Asia. Changing sea levels flooded many areas that are now land, changing them to shallow lagoons.

Atlantic Ocean

Armoured
Euoplocephalus was so well-armoured, even its eyelids had 'shutters' of bone.

'Hammer' at the end of the tail

Euoplocephalus [71]
you-OH-plo-kef-ah-luss
'Well-armoured head' was indeed well-protected all over. Fossilized bones and other parts from more than 40 individuals of this ankylosaur (armoured dinosaur) have been found in Midwestern North America. They suggest that this plant eater was up to 7 m long and 2 tonnes in weight. Its main defence was a heavy 'hammer' at the end of the tail, formed by four enlarged bones the size of basketballs.

Thick layer of bone
for head-butting

Stegoceras [76]
ste-GOS-er-as

One of the last groups of dinosaurs to appear were the plant-eating pachycephalosaurs or 'thick-headed reptiles'. They are often called 'boneheads' because of the very thick layer of bone forming the top of the skull, like a motorcyclist's crash-helmet. *Stegoceras*, 'roof horn', was only 2 m long and hardly a metre tall. Its fossils are North American. It may have had head-butting or head-ramming contests with others of its kind, like sheep and goats today during the breeding season. But the bone of the skull roof was lightweight and fairly spongy, and would soon be damaged by such physical battles.

Corythosaurus [68]
koh-rith-OH-sore-us

This large hadrosaur (duckbilled dinosaur) grew to 10 m long and almost 4 tonnes in weight. Its fossils are found mainly in Alberta, Canada and Montana, USA. Its name 'helmet reptile' refers to the shape of the bony head crest, which resembled the helmets of soldiers in Corinth, ancient Greece. Hadrosaurs had strong back legs and also sizeable front legs. They could probably lope along on all fours or rear up on their hind limbs to feed or sprint.

Richest
Rocks formed at the very end of the Cretaceous Period, 65 million years ago, are rich in iridium – a metal that is rare on Earth, but much more common in meteorites.

Albertosaurus [66]
al-BERT-oh-sore-us

This smaller and slightly earlier cousin of *Tyrannosaurus*, 'Alberta reptile' may have hunted young plant-eating dinosaurs such as hadrosaurs, or perhaps scavenged on the dead bodies of adults. *Albertosaurus* was about 9 m long and weighed perhaps 3 tonnes. Like its huge relative it had tiny, seemingly useless arms, each with a two-fingered hand.

Edmontonia [69]
ed-mon-TONE-ee-ah

Not to be confused with the duckbilled *Edmontosaurus*, this armoured dinosaur or ankylosaur belonged to the sub-group called nodosaurids. These lacked the large bony lumps at the end of the tail, like a club or hammer, to swing at enemies, which were a feature of the ankylosaurids such as *Euoplocephalus* (page 35). *Edmontonia*, 'from Edmonton', might charge and jab attackers with its neck and shoulder spikes. It was 7 m in length, and because of its armour, it probably weighed 4 tonnes.

Fastest
Studies of the leg bones of *Struthiomimus* indicate it could probably run as fast as an ostrich, at more than 80 km/h.

Struthiomimus [77]
strew-thee-oh-MEE-mus

One of the ostrich-dinosaurs, 'ostrich mimic' was similar in overall size and shape to a modern ostrich. Its long bony tail gave a total length of 4 m, and its powerful, sharp-clawed hands would be able to scratch, grasp and dig well. The beaklike mouth had no teeth at all. *Struthiomimus* probably pecked at all kinds of foods, from seeds and fruits to grubs, eggs and small mammals or reptiles. Its fossils come mainly from Alberta, Canada.

Trickiest
There are many ideas about why the dinosaurs, pterosaurs and other life forms disappeared in the mass extinction. But explaining how other creatures survived, such as crocodiles and turtles, is much more tricky.

Pteranodon [74]
tur-RAN-o-don
One of the largest and last pterosaurs, 'no-toothed wing' soared above central North America at the end of the Age of Dinosaurs. Its wings measured 10 m from tip-to-tip, and its tall pointed head crest resembled a thin witch's hat. The crest may have helped *Pteranodon* balance and steer as it flew. The beak and crest together measured almost 2 m.

Therizinosaurus [78]
THER-ih-zine-oh-SORE-us
One of the therizinosaurs or 'scythe reptiles', this massive dinosaur resembled its earlier cousin *Beipiaosaurus* (page 30). The reason for the huge hand claws remains a mystery – pulling down vegetation, ripping up nests of ants and termites, self-defence and many other reasons have been suggested. *Therizinosaurus* had a long giraffe-like neck and a toothless beaklike front to its mouth. It was 12 m in length and weighed two or more tonnes. It probably walked semi-upright on its rear limbs but its food remains a mystery.

Lambeosaurus [72]
lam-BEE-oh-SORE-us
The duckbilled dinosaurs were nicknamed from the wide, flat, toothless front of the mouth, similar to a duck's beak (bill). This gathered in foliage as food, which was crushed to a pulp by rows of hundreds of sharp-ridged cheek teeth. *Lambeosaurus* was 15 m long and lived in the Midwest of North America. Its fossils have also been found far to the southwest in Baja, California.

Bird or dinosaur?
Some experts say that since birds descended from dinosaurs they are not a separate group, and they should be regarded as living, feathered dinosaurs.

Avimimus [67]
ah-vee-MEEM-us
'Bird mimic' was a small theropod (carnivorous dinosaur) about 1.5 m long, and very light, at only 10 kg. Its strong, sharp beak pecked for food of small animals and perhaps plants. Some clues in the fossil bones suggest that *Avimimus* had feathers, at least on its front limbs. But these limbs were too small and weak to work as wings for flight. *Avimimus* lived in what is now the Gobi Desert of Mongolia.

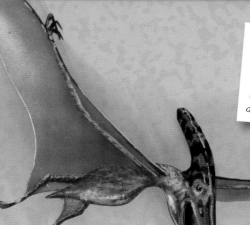

REASONS FOR DEATH

Why did the dinosaurs disappear?
Many reasons have been proposed for the mass extinction at the end of the Cretaceous Period. Most involve a huge meteorite or asteroid, perhaps 10 km across from outer space, which slammed into Earth. This would have thrown up vast amounts of dust and debris, which darkened the skies and led to global cooling and lack of plant food for herbivorous dinosaurs and other animals. The impact could also have set off tsunamis, or giant waves, earthquakes, and volcanic eruptions that poured poisonous gases into the atmosphere, adding to the mayhem.

DISCOVERING DINOSAURS

We know about dinosaurs because of their fossils. These are their bodily remains that were buried after death in mud, sand or similar materials. They were then preserved in rocks over millions of years, and gradually turned to stone. Not only dinosaurs, but many kinds of plants and animals have left fossils. These include shellfish, fish, amphibians, birds, mammals, insects, snails, and plants such as ferns and trees. Even microscopic pollen grains from flowers and tiny creatures floating in sea plankton can form fossils.

Which parts fossilize?

Usually only the hardest parts of living things form fos: For dinosaurs these are mainly bones, teeth, horns and claws. The softer parts such as muscles, nerves and even skin were soon consumed by scavengers or rotted away. However, fossilized dinosaur dung has been discovered. These fossils are called coprolites. Harder body parts were buried by silt, mud or sand, usually in water – a river, lake or sea. Since dinosaurs were land animals, their fossils are not as common as those of water creatures such as fish and shellfish. Usually only dinosaurs that drowned, or died on land and were then washed into a river or lake, ended up as fossils.

Coprolites – dinosaur dung

A chance-ridden process

The process of forming fossils is full of chance and subject to random events. The vast majority of dinosaur remains rotted and disappeared. Only a small proportion were preserved as fossils deep in rocks. Then more chance events determine whether the rocks are worn away to reveal the fossils at the surface, and also whether these fossils are ever seen, identified and collected by fossil-hunters.

Fossil clues

A fossilized claw of Baryonyx. Even fossils such as this provide palaeontologists (scientists who study fossilized remains) with huge amounts of information about the way a dinosaur lived – and what it may have looked like.

Dinosaur habitats

How do we know about the habitats dinosaurs lived in? Did a particular dinosaur prefer scattered woodland, dry scrub or thick forest? Palaeo-ecology is the study of all the fossils found in an area, not only from dinosaurs, but also the remains of other animals, tree bark, plant pollen and many other specimens. By combining these finds we can rebuild various types of habitats where dinosaurs lived, and try to understand how the dinosaurs interacted with other creatures and the environment of the time.

LOOKING AT DINOSAURS

What colour were dinosaurs?

Fossils are not original living material, but rock and stone, made of minerals. So a fossil's colour is that of its minerals. This means we cannot tell the colours of dinosaurs or other long-extinct animals from their fossils. Some dinosaurs may have been camouflaged in dull browns and greens, like living alligators and turtles. But others may have been bright and colourful, like some kinds of lizards and snakes are today. To produce lifelike models and pictures, such as those in this book, colours are chosen by intelligent guesswork and comparisons with living reptiles.

Stegosaurus may have had brightly coloured skin

Digging for dinosaurs

Scientists study rocks to find out their type and age. Dinosaur fossils occur in the sedimentary rocks of the Mesozoic Era – the Age of Dinosaurs. Palaeontologists then survey an area to establish if fossils are present. If remains are discovered, they dig and chip out the fossils with extreme care. They use many different kinds of tools and equipment ranging from ground-penetrating radar and jackhammer drills to hammers and chisels, scrapers, dental picks – and even soft brushes for delicate rocks. Every stage of the excavation or 'dig' is recorded with highly detailed notes, drawings, diagrams and photographs.

1. Digging
First, palaeontologists chip away rock covering the fossil. They may have to cut a deep trench in the surrounding rock to free the fossil.

2. Recording
Detailed diagrams and maps of the fossil positions are drawn up before any fossils are moved. These act as important documents when fossils are back in the laboratory.

3. Moving
Some fossils are carefully wrapped to protect them on their journey from the fossil site back to the laboratory.

Rebuilding dinosaurs

Back at the laboratory, staff clean and study the fossils with extreme care and patience. It is incredibly rare to find a full fossil skeleton of a dinosaur, with all the bones neatly arranged as they were in life. Usually the remains are squashed, crushed and broken, with parts fragmented and missing, and fossils of other living things mixed in and jumbled up. Great skill is needed to piece the fossils back together. Often fossils from other, similar types of dinosaurs are used to fill in missing parts or 'blanks'.

Bringing back to life

Once a dinosaur skeleton is reconstructed as far as possible, experts can begin to guess how it looked in life. Marks on the fossil bones called muscle scars show where muscles were attached, their sizes and lines of pull. Studies of dinosaur cousins alive today, such as crocodiles, lizards and birds, are used for comparison of soft parts like muscles and guts. Gradually the fossil skeleton is cloaked in flesh. Rare fossils of skin help to recreate the external appearance.

DINOSAURIA

Dinosaurs form a large group called the Dinosauria in the reptile 'supergroup', class Reptilia. The Dinosauria is divided into two subgroups known as Saurischia and Ornithischia, mainly on the basis of hip structure. Each group is subdivided in the same way that animals today are classified into groups.

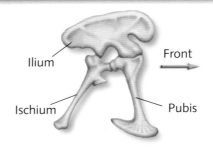

Ilium

Front

Ischium

Pubis

In the Saurischia or 'lizard-hips' (left), the projecting strut of the hip bone, known as the pubis, is angled down and forwards.

SAURISCHIA (lizard-hips)

This group of dinosaurs includes both meat eaters and plant eaters

THEROPODS (beast-feet)
Nearly all meat eaters, most walking on two legs, with three toes on each foot

HERRERASAURIDS *Herrerasaurus* and other very early meat eaters
CERATOSAURS *Dilophosaurus • Coelophysis*
ABELISAURS *Carnotaurus • Indoschus • Majungatholus*
EARLY TETANURANS (stiff-tails) *Megalosaurus • Eustreptospondylus*
SPINOSAURS *Baryonyx • Spinosaurus • Suchomimus*
ALLOSAURS *Allosaurus • Giganotosaurus • Caracharodontosaurus*
COELUROSAURS *Compsognathus • Ornitholestes • Sinosauropteryx*
ORNITHOMIMOSAURS (ostrich dinosaurs) *Gallimimus • Struthiomimus*
TYRANNOSAURS *Tyrannosaurus • Albertosaurus • Alectrosaurus*
THERIZINOSAURS (scythe lizards) *Therizinosaurus • Beipiaosaurus*
   (possibly the only plant-eating theropods)
OVIRAPTOSAURS *Oviraptor • Ingenia*
CAUDIPTERIDS *Caudipteryx*
DROMAEOSAURS (raptors) *Deinonychus • Velociraptor • Utahraptor*
MANIRAPTORANS *Troodon • Bambiraptor • Saurornithoides*
BIRDS *Archaeopteryx • Confuciusornis*

Herrerasaurus

Troodon

SAUROPODS (lizard-feet)
All plant eaters, most with long necks, bulky bodies, long tails and pillar-like feet

PROSAUROPODS *Plateosaurus • Riojasaurus • Massospondylus • Sellosaurus*
EARLY SAUROPODS *Vulcanodon • Barapasaurus • Cetiosaurus • Shunosaurus*
DICRAEOSAURS *Dicraeosaurus*
DIPLODOCIDS *Diplodocus • Apatosaurus • Barosaurus*
CAMARASAURS *Camarasaurus • Aragosaurus • Opisthocoelicaudia*
BRACHIOSAURS *Brachiosaurus • Bothriospondylus*
TITANOSAURS *Argentinosaurus • Saltasaurus • Nequensaurus*

Shunosaurus

In the Ornithischia or 'bird-hips' (right), the pubis angles down and rearwards.

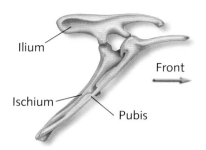

Ilium

Front

Ischium

Pubis

ORNITHISCHIA (bird-hips)

This group of dinosaurs is made up of just plant eaters, as far as is known

EARLY ORNITHISCHIANS
Pisanosaurus • Lesothosaurus • Gongbusaurus

THYREOPHORANS (shield-bearers)
EARLY THYREOPHORANS *Scelidosaurus • Scutellosaurus • Emausaurus*
STEGOSAURS *Stegosaurus • Kentrosaurus • Tuojiangosaurus*
ANKYLOSAURS (armoured dinosaurs, fused reptiles)
NODOSAURIDS (without tail club) *Edmontonia • Sauropelta • Panoplosaurus*
   ANKYLOSAURIDS (with tail club) *Euoplocephalus*
   POLACANTHIDS *Polacanthus*

Edmontonia

HETERODONTOSAURS (sometimes included in Ornithopods) *Heterodontosaurus*

HYPSILOPHODONTS (sometimes included in Ornithopods) *Hypsilophodon*

ORNITHOPODS (bird-feet)
DRYOSAURS *Dryosaurus*
CAMPTOSAURS *Camptosaurus • Callovosaurus*
IGUANODONTS *Iguanodon • Ouranosaurus • Altirhinus*
HADROSAURS (duckbills)
   HADROSAURINES (mostly without head-crests) *Hadrosaurus • Anatosaurus • Maiasaura • Edmontosaurus*
   LAMBEOSAURINES (mostly with head-crests) *Saurolophus • Parasaurolophus • Corythosaurus • Lambeosaurus*

Maiasaura

PACHYCEPHALOSAURS (thick-heads)
Pachycephalosaurus • Prenocephale • Stegoceras

Stegoceras

CERATOPSIANS (horn-faces)
PSITTACOSAURS *Psittacosaurus • Stenopelix*
PROTOCERATOPSIANS *Protoceratops • Breviceratops • Leptoceratops*
CERATOPSIANS
   CHASMOSAURINES (mostly small brow horns, large nose horn) *Chasmosaurus • Triceratops* (an exception)
   CENTROSAURINES (mostly large brow horns, small nose horn) *Centrosaurus • Styracosaurus*

PLANET DINOSAUR TODAY

In one sense, dinosaurs are still with us today. Around the world palaeontologists work at hundreds of fossil sites. Some are rich in fossils that have been known about for over a century, especially in Europe and the American Midwest. Others have come to light during the past few years, such as the finds of feathered dinosaurs in China. Fresh discoveries force experts to revise their ideas and generate new ones about how these creatures lived and died. This world map shows where some dinosaur remains have been excavated. All of these dinosaurs can be found in this book.

NORTH AMERICA

Alberta, Canada: *Lambeosaurus* [72]
Alaska, USA: *Parasaurolophus* [73]
Colorado, USA: *Apatosaurus* [35]
Montana, USA: *Deinonychus* [53]
Utah, USA: *Allosaurus* [34]

Lambeosaurus

Parasaurolophus

Apatosaurus

Deinonychus

Allosaurus

SOUTH AMERICA

Cerro Rajada, Argentina: *Riojasaurus* [11]
El Breté, Argentina: *Saltasaurus* [75]
Bolivia: *Triceratops* tracks [79]
Santa Maria, Brazil: *Staurikosaurus* [14]

Riojasaurus

Triceratops

Saltasaurus

Staurikosaurus

EUROPE

Belgium: *Megalosaurus* [26]
Isle of Wight, England: *Iguanodon* [56]
Solnhofen, Germany: *Archaeopteryx* [36]
Trossingen, Germany: *Plateosaurus* [9]

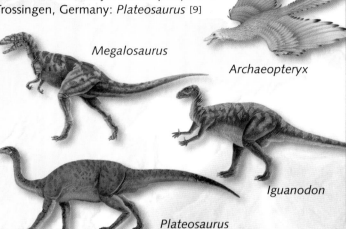

Megalosaurus

Archaeopteryx

Iguanodon

Plateosaurus

ASIA

China: *Caudipteryx* [52], *Tuojiangosaurus* [48]
Mongolia: *Psittacosaurus* [62]

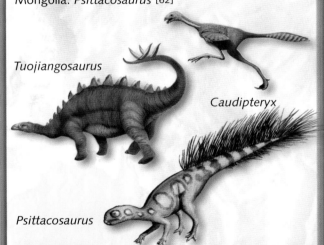

Tuojiangosaurus

Caudipteryx

Psittacosaurus

AFRICA

Lesotho, Southern Africa: *Lesothosaurus* [25]
Tanzania: *Brachiosaurus* [37]

Lesothosaurus

Brachiosaurus

OCEANIA

Queensland, Australia: *Minmi* [59]
Victoria, Australia: *Leaellynasaura* [57]

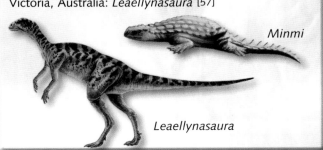

Minmi

Leaellynasaura

DINOSAUR FINDER

Below is a key to the five main scenes within the book.
Use this as a guide to finding and naming every dinosaur.

THE DINOSAURS ARRIVE

1 Coelophysis
2 Eoraptor
3 Eudimorphodon
4 Herrerasaurus
5 Massospondylus
6 Melanorosaurus
7 Mussaurus
8 Ornithosuchus
9 Plateosaurus
10 Procompsognathus
11 Riojasaurus
12 Saltopus
13 Scaphonyx
14 Staurikosaurus
15 Thecodontosaurus
16 Thrinaxodon

BIGGER AND FIERCER

17 Anchisaurus
18 Barapasaurus
19 Barosaurus
20 Cetiosaurus
21 Dilophosaurus
22 Dimorphodon
23 Eustreptospondylus
24 Heterodontosaurus
25 Lesothosaurus
26 Megalosaurus
27 Megazostrodon
28 Rhoetosaurus
29 Scelidosaurus
30 Scutellosaurus
31 Seismosaurus
32 Shunosaurus
33 Yunnanosaurus

THE MEGA-SAURS

34 *Allosaurus*
35 *Apatosaurus*
36 *Archaeopteryx*
37 *Brachiosaurus*
38 *Camarasaurus*
39 *Ceratosaurus*
40 *Coelurus*
41 *Compsognathus*
42 *Diplodocus*
43 *Kentrosaurus*
44 *Mamenchisaurus*
45 *Ornitholestes*
46 *Rhamphorhynchus*
47 *Sauroposeidon*
48 *Tuojiangosaurus*

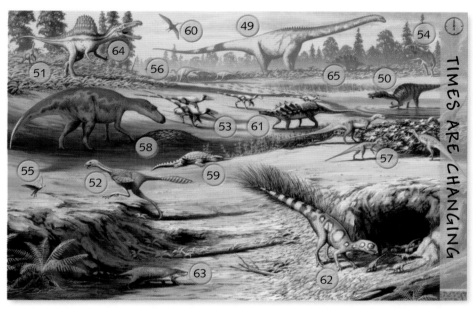

TIMES ARE CHANGING

49 *Argentinosaurus*
50 *Baryonyx*
51 *Beipiaosaurus*
52 *Caudipteryx*
53 *Deinonychus*
54 *Giganotosaurus*
55 *Iberomesornis*
56 *Iguanodon*
57 *Leaellynasaura*
58 *Maiasaura*
59 *Minmi*
60 *Ornithodesmus*
61 *Polacanthus*
62 *Psittacosaurus*
63 *Repenomamus robustus*
64 *Spinosaurus*
65 *Stegosaurus*

THE END IS NEAR

66 *Albertosaurus*
67 *Avimimus*
68 *Corythosaurus*
69 *Edmontonia*
70 *Edmontosaurus*
71 *Euoplocephalus*
72 *Lambeosaurus*
73 *Parasaurolophus*
74 *Pteranodon*
75 *Saltasaurus*
76 *Stegoceras*
77 *Struthiomimus*
78 *Therizinosaurus*
79 *Triceratops*
80 *Troodon*
81 *Tyrannosaurus*
82 *Zalambdalestes*

INDEX